KU-410-002

Real
Life
GUIDES

WORKING WITH
ANIMALS AND WILDLIFE

REAL LIFE GUIDES

Practical guides for practical people

In this increasingly sophisticated world the need for manually skilled people to build our homes, cut our hair, fix our boilers, and make our cars go is greater than ever. As things progress, so the level of training and competence required of our skilled manual workers increases.

In this new series of career guides from Trotman, we look in detail at what it takes to train for, get into, and be successful at a wide spectrum of practical careers. The *Real Life Guides* aim to inform and inspire young people and adults alike by providing comprehensive yet hard-hitting and often blunt information about what it takes to succeed in these careers.

Other titles in the series are:

Real Life Guide: The Armed Forces
Real Life Guide: The Beauty Industry
Real Life Guide: Carpentry & Cabinet-Making
Real Life Guide: Catering
Real Life Guide: Construction
Real Life Guide: Electrician
Real Life Guide: Hairdressing
Real Life Guide: The Motor Industry
Real Life Guide: Plumbing
Real Life Guide: The Police Force
Real Life Guide: Retailing
Real Life Guide: Working Outdoors
Real Life Guide: Working with Young People

trotman

Real Life GUIDES

WORKING WITH
ANIMALS AND WILDLIFE

Brin Best and
Felicity Haynes

Real Life Guide to Working with Animals and Wildlife
This first edition published in 2005 by Trotman and Company Ltd
2 The Green, Richmond, Surrey TW9 1PL

© Trotman and Company Limited 2005

Reprinted 2006

Editorial and Publishing Team
Authors Brin Best and Felicity Haynes
Editorial Mina Patria, Editorial Director; Rachel Lockhart,
Commissioning Editor; Catherine Travers, Managing Editor;
Ian Turner, Editorial Assistant
Production Ken Ruskin, Head of Manufacturing and
Logistics; James Rudge, Production Artworker
Sales and Marketing Suzanne Johnson, Marketing
Manager
Advertising Tom Lee, Commercial Director

Designed by XAB

British Library Cataloguing in Publications Data
A catalogue record for this book is available from the British
Library

ISBN 978 1 84455 053 1

Typeset by Photoprint, Torquay
Printed and bound in Great Britain by
The Cromwell Press, Trowbridge, Wiltshire

Real Life

GUIDES

CONTENTS

ABOUT THE AUTHORS	VII
ACKNOWLEDGEMENTS	IX
INTRODUCTION	1
1. REAL LIVES 1	8
2. WHAT'S THE STORY?	13
3. CASE STUDY 1	17
4. WHAT JOBS ARE AVAILABLE?	23
5. REAL LIVES 2	33
6. TOOLS OF THE TRADE	45
7. CHALLENGES TO CONSIDER	53
8. TRAINING DAY	58
9. CASE STUDY 2	68
10. GETTING A JOB	72
11. CASE STUDY 3	77
12. CASE STUDY 4	81
13. MAKING UP YOUR MIND	84
14. THE LAST WORD	88
15. RESOURCES	91

About the authors

Brin Best is the Director of Innovation *for* Education Ltd, an education training and consultancy company based in Yorkshire. He has a degree in environmental sciences and is a qualified teacher. Prior to his work as a teacher and education adviser, he worked in wildlife conservation as a marine ornithologist and tropical rainforest researcher. Brin has written or edited 14 other books on topics ranging from tropical forest ecology to the wildlife of the Yorkshire Dales. He is very active as a volunteer within wildlife organisations, and is a trustee of the Royal Society for the Protection of Birds and the Wharfedale Naturalists' Society.

Felicity Haynes runs a tack shop in the Yorkshire Dales with her partner, and they have both been involved with animals and animal care all their lives. Felicity has a degree in geography and health studies and is currently working part-time in a school as a teaching assistant, as well as writing on a freelance basis. Her main passion is horses, and she is a regular competitor in riding competitions. She enjoys driving her pony around the quiet lanes of the Yorkshire Dales in a two-wheeled cart, and keeps a variety of pets including dogs, cats and guinea pigs. Felicity is keen to inspire young people to pursue a career working with animals and wildlife.

Acknowledgements

We are very grateful to all those people who agreed to be interviewed for this book – their support made the project possible and enriched the text considerably. We would like to thank Anne Harley, director of human resources at the Royal Society for the Protection of Birds (RSPB), who provided valuable comments that helped us improve the book. Anne also put us in touch with Sally Mills, site manager at Ham Wall RSPB reserve. Useful information came from the press offices of English Nature and World Wildlife Fund (WWF) UK. Gill O'Donnell and Rosie Haynes provided helpful comments on an earlier draft of this book and Mina Patria and Rachel Lockhart provided valuable editorial support in the Trotman office.

Introduction

What images come to mind when you think about working with animals?

- Carrying out lifesaving operations on sick animals?
- Training guide dogs to help transform the lives of blind people?
- Protecting endangered birds on pristine nature reserves?
- Helping to run a small organic farm?

Working with animals and wildlife certainly offers a wide range of exciting and rewarding opportunities: this book will help you consider them in detail.

You are probably reading this because you already have an interest in animals or wildlife and want to know more about how you can make it into a career. If so, you have come to the right place, as this book is designed to help you make sensible choices about the next steps you can take.

The employment sector linked to working with animals and wildlife is currently booming, so there has never been a better time to enter the sector.

IT'S NOT ALL CUDDLY ANIMALS AND LONG DAYS IN THE SUN

Working with animals and wildlife can be very rewarding, but before you read any further you need to be aware that it also has its fair share of challenges. Long hours, dirt, sweat, blood and tears ... all are guaranteed at some point in the

DID YOU KNOW?

1.5 million people work in the environmental and land-based sector in the UK, and over 25,000 new people will be needed in the next five years.

job. Because of this, a key point to bear in mind is that you must be really determined if you want to pursue a career working in this sector. You also need to really care about animals and wildlife without being too sentimental about them, and this can be a difficult balance to achieve.

Having said that, the rewards are certainly there if you can rise to the challenge. You could find yourself seeing wounded animals through to a successful recovery, working in spectacular scenery with exotic wildlife in the Ecuadorian rainforests or feeling incredibly proud when a horse that you have spent months training wins a show-jumping competition.

You need to really care about animals and wildlife without being too sentimental about them, and this can be a difficult balance to achieve.

WHAT TYPES OF JOBS ARE ON OFFER?
There are six main categories of work with animals and wildlife:

- **Animal health and welfare** – including occupations like physiotherapist, vet, animal behaviourist, dog warden, alternative therapist and animal technician

- **Animal care charities** – including work at rescue centres and/or for organisations such as the Royal Society for the Prevention of Cruelty to Animals (RSPCA)
- **Wildlife management and conservation** – including work to protect species or habitats for charities such as the Royal Society for the Protection of Birds (RSPB) in jobs like farm wildlife adviser, ecologist, scientific researcher and gamekeeper
- **The animal and wildlife business** – including jobs like farmer, fish-farmer, auctioneer, riding instructor, falconer, river bailiff or animal breeder/trainer in locations such as horse studs, kennels and catteries, zoos and the countryside. This area also includes wildlife entertainment and tourism
- **Services provided through animals** – including work as a dog handler for the police, customs or the mounted police
- **Indirect animal and wildlife occupations** – including animal nutrition, working in a pet food shop, tack shop or feed merchants or educating people about animals and wildlife.

Each of these categories is explored in more detail in Chapter 4. This book will focus most on those professions that have direct contact with animals and wildlife, thereby touching only briefly on the last category. We will also stay clear of those jobs involving animals that are not alive (eg taxidermist, pest control officer, slaughterhouse worker etc).

WHO CAN YOU WORK FOR?

One of the advantages of a career working with animals or wildlife is that it is possible to find employment in a huge range of different situations. As shown by the list of job types on the previous page, it is possible to work for employers as diverse as:

- Government agencies such as the Environment Agency or English Nature (the latter organisation will be renamed 'Natural England' in 2006)
- National or local charities, such as the RSPCA and the county Wildlife Trusts
- Private companies or individuals providing relevant products and services
- Yourself (ie being self-employed).

The kind of work you undertake within these different sectors can be radically different too, and many of the jobs give you the chance to work with other colleagues and with the general public. Whatever type of job you focus on, you are sure to develop a wide range of useful skills along the way, which will be transferable to other careers.

It is also worth noting that some of the jobs listed above are quite competitive and some need very specific qualifications. For example, a lot of young people are interested in marine biology or veterinary science, but not everyone can get the A level grades needed to study these subjects at university. Make sure you are realistic about what you can achieve.

WHERE CAN YOU WORK?
You will be pleased to hear that for many of the jobs that involve working with animals or wildlife you can more or less take your pick of where to live and work. There are opportunities in every part of the UK, in built-up as well as rural areas.

Even if you choose a career in wildlife conservation, you should not rule out getting a job in a city. Many of our best nature reserves are now located in urban areas – for example, the award-winning London Wetland Centre, which protects over 40 hectares of specially created wetland in the heart of London. Although only established in 2000, this Wildfowl and Wetlands Trust Reserve is already a Site of Special Scientific Interest (SSSI), supporting nationally important numbers of ducks.

Of course many people working with animals or wildlife love the wild outdoors too. Working in this sector will certainly give you the chance to live and work in some of the most outstanding natural areas of the UK, or even overseas.

DID YOU KNOW?

At the end of March 2004 there were 215 National Nature Reserves in England covering 87,900 hectares. Reserves can be found scattered through England from Lindisfarne in Northumberland to the Lizard Peninsula in Cornwall. Nearly every rural community has at least one.

HOW THIS BOOK WILL HELP

This book will guide you through the various career routes to consider if you are thinking of working with animals or wildlife. It will also give you the chance to think more deeply about whether this really is a job area for you.

Throughout the book there are in-depth interviews with people who already work with animals and wildlife in the 'Case Studies' and 'Real Lives' chapters. Like you, at some point in their lives the people interviewed in this book felt the desire to seriously consider this career option, and those featured stuck with it and now get paid to work with animals and wildlife.

We firmly believe that you can learn a huge amount by talking to those who are out there doing the work, and we hope the interviews and case studies in this book will help you build up a more comprehensive picture of what daily life is like working with animals and wildlife. Below is a list of interviews featured in this book:

Sue Allstack	Kennels and cattery owner	page 8
David Elms	Tack shop owner	page 9
Adrian Procter	Organic farmer	page 11
Sally Mills	Nature reserve site manager	page 17
Florus Oskam	Vet	page 33
Kayleigh McIntyre	Trainee veterinary nurse	page 35
Gavin Clunie	Animal carer	page 38
Jenny Holden	Owl charity conservation officer	page 41
Amanda Best	Biodiversity officer	page 68
Dr Piran White	University ecology lecturer	page 77
Karen Rushton-Wright	Groom	page 81

We have also included a quiz to help you gauge how much you already know about animals and wildlife. At the end of the book is a section on resources, which will show you where to go to find out more.

TIME FOR REFLECTION

It is a good idea to pause at this stage and consider a few important questions that will help you get the most out of this book:

- What do you already know about careers with animals and wildlife? (You can use the quiz on page 47 to test yourself on this.)
- What specifically do you want to find out from this book?
- Which types of jobs, if any, have you already considered?

The key message we want to put across is that the best thing you can do to ensure that you are making the right choice is to carry out plenty of research before taking any major steps. This book will help you to begin this process.

Real lives 1

SUE ALLSTACK – KENNELS AND CATTERY OWNER

Sue Allstack owns Hallstack Kennels and Cattery near Settle, North Yorkshire.

Why did you decide to open a boarding kennels and cattery?
'I had a two-year-old Labrador dog. A friend saw it one day and said I ought to start showing it. I then got myself another dog. I'd worked at a dairy for 21 years and I was sick of it so handed in my notice. I wanted to work from home so decided that I had enough room to build and started Hallstack Kennels and Cattery.'

How many dogs and cats can you take?
'I'm licensed to have 30 dogs and 20 cats. The numbers vary but it tends not to be seasonal as people go on holidays at all times of the year.'

What hours do you work during an average week?
'Like farming, this job is a way of life. The kennels are open from 8am until 8pm seven days a week. Sometimes customers ring me at 11.30pm to book their dog or cat in.'

> 'Get as much experience with animals as you can, even if it's just walking dogs. Experience is one of the most important things.'

What are the highs and lows of the job?
'I really enjoy working with the animals – but it's hard if an animal is ill and I find it upsetting when a customer rings to say their dog has died.'

What advice would you give somebody wanting to pursue a career in this field?
'Get as much experience with animals as you can, even if it's just walking dogs. Experience is one of the most important things.'

What are the important personal qualities?
'To be animal-orientated, caring, calm and responsible. Confidence is another important quality but this grows with experience. As you're dealing with the public, people skills are vital too. Generally speaking, if you love animals there shouldn't be a problem.'

DAVID ELMS – TACK SHOP OWNER
David Elms runs a tack shop business with his partner as well as working part time on a smallholding in the Yorkshire Dales.

Have you always wanted to work with animals?
'Yes, I have. Initially I wanted to train as a veterinary surgeon, but was not able to get the grades that were required to get on the course.'

What training have you had?
'After leaving school at 16, I went to Askham Bryan College to do a National Diploma in Horse Studies. Whilst there I also completed Horse Owner's Certificates 1, 2 and 3, the British Horse Society Stage 1 qualification and the Riding and Road Safety Certificate.'

What hours do you do in a typical week?
'I spend 25 hours a week working in the shop, and the rest of my time I spend on a smallholding with horses and sheep. I work on average 65 hours a week, but this does go up or down depending on the season.'

What are the highs and the lows of having a tack shop business?
'The highs would be that I get to meet new people, and I'm selling products that I'm interested in. The lows of the job are that money is tight, as most people discover when they first set up a business, and this is made worse when you have quiet days and you have to sit there on your own.'

Take your time and don't rush into anything.

Do salary levels reflect the work you have to do with the business?
'We have only just come to the end of our first year in business, and salary levels have not reflected the hours of work put in.'

What advice would you give someone interested in starting their own business?
'You definitely need to have a sound knowledge in your subject area. You also need to have some kind of financial backing. Make sure that you do your groundwork before you start; talk to people already in that business, and get advice from a business adviser. Most importantly, take your time and don't rush into anything.'

ADRIAN PROCTER – ORGANIC FARMER

Adrian Procter is an organic farmer who has a farm near Settle, North Yorkshire.

Have you always had an interest in animals?
'Yes I have. I was brought up on a farm so have been used to animals right from the word go.'

When did you decide that you wanted to be a farmer?
'I drifted into it. I worked on the farm as a child, and carried on from there.'

Did you ever consider any other jobs?
'I did think that if I hadn't gone into farming I would have been a mechanic or an engineer, and I've always enjoyed building.'

Have you done any training?
'Yes – I did three years' day release to gain a qualification as an agricultural craftsman. You learn a lot from your peers and there's no substitute for experience.'

What hours do you do in a typical week?
'I work on average 60 hours per week.'

What are the highs and lows of the job?
'The highs of the job would have to be that I work in an attractive area, don't have to commute and I'm my own boss. The lows of the job are the piles of paperwork I have to do and the weather when it's against you. These days a lot is driven by the supermarkets, and they can get cheaper imports but not always to the same standard.'

What skills do you think are important for the job?
'You need to have a variety of skills, including plumbing and building; sometimes it's like being a handyman really. You also need to be able to do book work and know something about animal illnesses and crops in different areas.'

What advice would you give someone interested in pursuing a career in this field?
'Firstly, you have to put in a lot of work for the return that you get. Unfortunately it's nearly impossible now for people to acquire their own farm if they're not from a farming background. But there are opportunities for people to become farm workers and herdspeople. This is a more viable option for someone not from a farming family, interested in a farming career. Wages are quite good for experienced people, with houses sometimes included to attract the right person. You need to be able to adapt to the market opportunities or government policies. You always have options as farming is a physical job and most farmers can adapt to different jobs, as they are practical.'

You need to be able to adapt to the market opportunities or government policies.

What are your plans for the future?
'My aim is to sell all my produce either locally or direct to the end user.'

What's the story?

2

This chapter will present some background information on working with animals and wildlife. It will help you understand some of the key issues affecting employment in this sector in the UK at the beginning of the Twenty-first Century.

ON THE UP

There is no doubt that you are considering a job sector that is on the rise. In the last 20 years there has been a big increase in the number of jobs available in the outdoor sector as a whole.

Employment linked to the environment and nature conservation in particular has risen sharply. The high profile Earth Summits of 1992, 1997 and 2002 have helped to put the spotlight on the need for sustainable development – making sure we use the Earth's resources sensibly today so that they are there for future generations to enjoy.

In the UK this has resulted in a range of new measures to safeguard our natural environment or to develop specific aspects of the economy. One example is the

DID YOU KNOW?

It is estimated that there are 47,000 paid employees working with animals and wildlife, and a further 200,000 volunteers.

England Rural Development Programme, which has injected £1.6 billion into the countryside to create jobs, enhance the rural economy and protect our natural heritage.

The UK is famous for being a nation of animal lovers. A large proportion of the population now has pets and needs to spend money on them, from dog grooming to veterinary expenses. Collectively the UK animal health market is worth about £360 million a year. The total market for cat and dog food alone is currently worth £1.6 billion per annum, with the market predicted to grow by around 12% by 2006.

The UK is famous for being a nation of animal lovers. A large proportion of the population now has pets and needs to spend money on them.

At the same time people's interest in animal welfare has mushroomed. New charities have been formed focusing on the need to take measures to protect specific habitats or species, such as our seas or the otter.

There has also been an upsurge in entertainment and tourism linked to animals and wildlife. This has presented new opportunities for work in zoos, wildlife tourism and in a range of other workplaces.

Some professions working with animals and wildlife, however, are oversubscribed. Take RSPCA inspectors, for example: there are over 2000 applicants a year for only 20 jobs. However, for some other types of jobs there is a real shortage of suitably qualified people, presenting an ideal opportunity for people who can target such professions. Wildlife survey skills, for example, fall into this category – there are too few new people available to fill the posts that exist now, not to mention those that may be created in the future.

TRAINING ROUTES AND PAY

Some jobs working with animals and wildlife do not require any specific qualifications – just bags of enthusiasm and commitment. But for a growing number of jobs in this sector, qualifications of one sort or another are needed. Education and training opportunities include GCSEs, A levels, HNDs, National Vocational Qualifications (NVQs) and apprenticeships, as well as higher-level qualifications such as degrees.

Pay rates are very variable, but in general you should not expect to get paid large amounts of money for working with animals and wildlife. The following is a rough guide to the range of wages on offer in this sector (remember that pay rates can vary in different areas and with different employers):

- A groom in a small stables can earn £10,000 a year
- A nature reserve warden can earn £15,000 a year

DID YOU KNOW?

In several English regions, zoos rank amongst the top ten tourist attractions for which admission is charged. In the past 50 years many zoos have transformed themselves from places where animals were crowded together in cramped cages to sites where important conservation work is carried out. The successful captive breeding of rare species such as giant pandas is just one example of the success of zoos.

- An experienced veterinary nurse can earn upwards of £18,000 a year
- An established ecologist working for a government agency can earn £23,000 a year
- A junior university lecturer can earn £25,000 a year
- A vet with experience in a large practice can earn upwards of £35,000 a year.

DID YOU KNOW?

The number of male veterinary nurses in the UK is barely in double figures, making this predominantly a female career.

Despite the old-fashioned stereotypes, employment prospects for men and women are good in all aspects of the sector. In jobs that were previously dominated by men, women are now catching up. The only barriers that remain are, therefore, in people's minds.

SALLY MILLS

Case study 1

3

NATURE RESERVE SITE MANAGER

Sally Mills works as the site manager at Ham Wall RSPB reserve near Glastonbury, Somerset, an internationally important wetland. The 190-hectare reserve has been created out of worked-out peat diggings to form a patchwork of pools and reed beds that attract a range of birds and other wildlife.

What's a typical day like?
'The most exciting part of my job is that no two days are ever the same, so a typical day is quite difficult to describe. However, tasks that could make up a spring/summer day may be:

- Getting up at dawn to carry out a bird survey recording the breeding birds on the reserve
- Fuelling and starting the generator to aerate the new ecopod composting scheme that we are currently running, which aims to convert cut reed and grass into compost
- Checking the animals (we currently have three water buffalo and 17 highland

Volunteering is a great way to get involved in this type of work and to gain experience of different management techniques and habitats.

cattle, which we need to count and check every day to ensure that they're all present and healthy)
- Getting back to the office to deal with any emails and administration, such as putting together budgets, planning applications, replying to enquiries and preparing for talks, meetings etc
- Going to see the contractor working for us undertaking wetland restoration. His work may involve putting in ground elevation levels with a theodolite so that he can re-profile the ground to the required heights needed for the establishment of different wetland habitats
- Liaising with staff and volunteers about work coming up
- If I haven't got up at dawn for a bird survey, then I might carry out practical work on the reserve, such as estate work (eg putting up gates or fences), creation work (eg planting reeds) or management work (eg cutting and removing vegetation)'.

When did you first become interested in wildlife?
'Birds have dominated my life really, and have a lot to answer for! As an adolescent they were an endless source of fascination. At college they got me into trouble for missing lectures. Over the years, they have drawn me to interesting places and to meet interesting people. Now they often make me a target of ridicule amongst my peers, especially my hockey team! But they're a way of life, and as site manager at Ham Wall, they've led me to my biggest challenge ever – the transformation of a peat-extracted landscape into a mosaic of wetland habitats. But they are worth it!'

What species do you work with?
'I don't work directly with birds, but I help to provide habitats for them – such as reed beds, open water, wet

scrub and grassland. These habitats benefit a variety of species, including endangered wetland birds like the bittern, marsh harrier and bearded tit, and some of our rarer mammals like the water vole and otter. The habitat creation and management work that we undertake on the reserve provides areas not just for rare wetland wildlife, but also for more widespread species such as the barn owl, stonechat and roe deer, and for a wide range of invertebrates and small mammals.'

Did you consider any other jobs?
'When I first left university, I became a freelance bird artist and sculptor and so was self-employed. The RSPB has been my one and only employer and since working for them on their nature reserves I've never wanted to consider other types of jobs.'

What hours do you work in an average week?
'This is a difficult one! My contract is written so that I will work the hours necessary to undertake the job – so I always work at least 9 hours per day. I regularly work 10-hour days and sometimes it can be as much as 12 hours. Lunchtime and coffee breaks only take place if I'm working with volunteers – otherwise, I work right through. I work at least one Sunday in a month, sometimes more – and getting that time off "in lieu" (in place of the extra days worked) often never happens. Life is busy and there's always plenty to do.'

DID YOU KNOW?

The water vole is threatened in the UK due to the introduced mink from the USA, which escaped from fur farms. Work is underway by organisations such as the Vincent Wildlife Trust to find ways of halting the decline.

The habitat creation and management work that we undertake on the reserve provides areas not just for rare wetland wildlife, but also for more widespread species.

What training do you have?
'I graduated in 1989, with a First Class BA (Hons) degree in Art. Then, after working on short-term contracts for the RSPB, I was offered a training post for three years, which involved working on three different reserves and studying for a Postgraduate Diploma (PgDip) in Environmental Conservation. This diploma involved all aspects of conservation work, including everything from practical skills like tractor driving, chainsaw operation and constructing boardwalks to academic skills like writing a management plan and conducting surveys. I was on short-term contracts for the RSPB for five years before securing my current permanent position, and this contract system was an excellent form of training. It enabled me to work on various reserves, gaining varied experience of different habitats and management methods, and acquiring a variety of skills such as dealing with the public, taking school groups and running events.'

What advice would you give somebody interested in pursuing a career in this field?
'You need to have a sound interest in the area in which you choose to work, and not be frightened of hard work and long hours. (However, the rewards are fantastic and well worth all the effort.) Volunteering is a great way to get involved in this type of work and to gain experience of

different management techniques and habitats. In fact, when applying for jobs it's pretty much essential to be able to include volunteering on your CV, as it helps to illustrate your commitment to conservation. It's a great field to get involved in, but it's a difficult one to find work in, with lots of competition. Often the defining factor will be the range of interests you have and the variety of experience you've managed to obtain.'

What are the highs and lows of the job?
'There are always highs and lows in any job. The lows are the amount of work to do and often the lack of resources to do it, the biting insects, the long hours and the reality of the bigger picture. The highs are seeing the reserve on a frosty, sunny morning, watching wildlife use areas that we have designed, created or managed, hearing the first bittern boom in a section of reed we established, watching the first wheelchair user test out the recycled plastic boardwalk that we installed, introducing grazing animals and seeing them venture into the reed bed, initiating new projects like composting, obtaining the relevant permissions and gaining funding for a big project, and getting a big task completed with the volunteers.'

What plans do you have for the future?
'To remain in conservation work for the RSPB and hopefully to stay working at grass roots level, probably on reserves, because that's what I enjoy doing most. To continue to try

> **DID YOU KNOW?**
>
> Ecology is now taught at many UK universities, despite only being introduced as a degree course in the last few decades. Several universities now offer specialist Master's degrees in Ecology and Conservation.

and make a difference, but to increase the scale, to influence people and to try to get nature conservation even higher on the list of priorities.'

The highs are seeing the reserve on a frosty, sunny morning, watching wildlife use areas that we have designed, created or managed, hearing the first bittern boom in a section of reed we established, watching the first wheelchair user test out the recycled plastic boardwalk that we installed...

What jobs are available?

4

This chapter provides an overview of the wide range of occupations that you can consider if you are interested in working with animals or wildlife. As explained in the introduction, the occupations in this book are divided up into six broad categories – but in reality there is some overlap between these categories.

ANIMAL HEALTH AND WELFARE

The animal health and welfare area is a very important part of the overall animal and wildlife sector. While a vets' practice may first come to mind, don't forget that there are many other jobs that fall into the category of animal health and welfare. They include animal behaviourists who work with problem pets, and dog wardens who round up strays from the streets.

Jobs linked to animal health and welfare are very varied and call for people working at a basic level right up to senior staff taking major decisions. Jobs available in this area include:

DID YOU KNOW?

Animal behaviourists work to help train 'naughty' pets or animals that are psychologically disturbed. The famous film with Robert Redford entitled *The Horse Whisperer* features a man known for his ability to cure injured and spiritually troubled horses.

- Vet
- Veterinary nurse
- Animal technician (caring for animals involved in research)
- Alternative therapist (working with sick animals using treatments such as homeopathy)
- Physiotherapist (helping animals overcome illness or problems with their movements)
- Animal behaviourist (helping animals overcome problem behaviours)
- Dog warden (rounding up stray dogs and helping to find them a home)
- Dog beautician (pampering pets).

If animal health and welfare is the career route you go down, you will need to be sympathetic and sensitive to the feelings of others as you will often be dealing with people who are distressed (because their animals are injured or sick).

ANIMAL CARE CHARITIES

There are many charities doing excellent work to care for animals and to find them a safe home, with some well-known examples being Cats Protection (CP) and the Dogs Trust. Jobs available in this area include:

- Looking after animals in a rescue centre as a veterinary nurse or animal carer
- Training animals so that they can become good pets
- Working with the public to educate people about pets
- Carrying out administrative or other office-based tasks such as fundraising to help run the charity
- Going out and about to find and save injured animals.

A job working with animal charities is bound to put you in contact with people, so good interpersonal and communication skills are essential. It is also worth noting that work of this type is often quite poorly paid, so it is not an area to go into if money really matters to you.

Enthusiasm, commitment and lots of initiative are needed for all jobs working with animals and wildlife.

WILDLIFE MANAGEMENT AND CONSERVATION

This is a big growth area, with extra government money being ploughed into environmental schemes. More and more charities are working to safeguard threatened habitats and species, with grants from the National Lottery and other sources helping to boost their cause.

If you are interested in working in wildlife management and conservation, then there are two main routes to go down:

- Hands-on work managing habitats and working with particular animals. Jobs available in this area include nature reserve warden, gamekeeper, nature conservation species officer, wildlife surveyor and farm wildlife adviser.
- More 'hands-off' work, which includes an increased element of office work and meetings. This could mean working with the public as an education officer, being an ecology researcher or working for a government agency.

The box below gives you an idea of the range of jobs available in a large wildlife conservation charity.

TEN JOBS WITH THE RSPB, EUROPE'S LARGEST CONSERVATION CHARITY

- Bird surveyor – carrying out counts and making observations of birds on reserves
- Director of conservation – making important decisions about the conservation policy of the charity
- Field teacher – working with children at nature reserves to help them learn more about birds
- Site manager – being in charge of one reserve and carrying out management to make it better for birds
- Photographer – taking photographs of birds and people for the magazine *Birds* and other publications
- Agricultural policy officer – advising staff on how agricultural issues affect birds and lobbying the government to improve prospects for birds in our countryside
- Head of public affairs – responsible for maintaining the public image of the society
- Special projects officer – working on a particular project or campaign that responds to the rapidly changing world of bird conservation
- Fundraising officer – working to raise funds so that the charity can continue its work
- Database coordinator – using IT skills to manage a large computer database on threatened species.

THE ANIMAL AND WILDLIFE BUSINESS

The animal business in the UK is a multi-million pound industry. There is a huge range of possible jobs to consider – from horse racing to fish farming, zoos to wildlife tourism. If you are a budding entrepreneur, this is the area to focus on, with opportunities for new businesses to sell products and services. Jobs available in this area include:

- Farmer and fish farmer
- Auctioneer
- Work with racehorses (including groomer, horse trainer and even jockey)
- Riding instructor and work in a horse stud (where horses are bred)
- River bailiff
- Animal breeder or trainer (including the breeding of show dogs, cats and other animals)
- Kennels and cattery work
- Zoo work (including zookeeper, management roles and work with the public in an education capacity)
- Falconer
- Wildlife entertainment and tourism work (including bird tour leader, specialist animal park worker or even having your own insect road show)
- Wildlife film-maker, writer or photographer.

> **DID YOU KNOW?**
>
> The RSPB is Europe's largest wildlife conservation charity, with over 1440 staff and in excess of 1 million members. It was voted one of the top 50 UK workplaces in a 2005 survey.

The jobs above are very diverse and require a variety of skills and levels of training. Not everyone is comfortable making money from animals, so you need to make sure you are happy with this concept before going any further.

SERVICES PROVIDED THROUGH ANIMALS

One of the wonders of animals is that, through their senses or by their sheer presence, they can really help people. Working with animals in this intimate way requires you to be very comfortable living and working with them. Some people seem to have a natural affinity with animals, and these are the people who would be most at home helping to provide such services as those listed below:

- Anybody who has seen a dog at work that has been specially trained to help blind or deaf people will never forget it. Animals can genuinely change, and even save, lives.

- Security concerns in recent years have meant that we often see sniffer dogs on our TV screens that are trained to root out explosives or drugs. Dogs also play a vital role in finding people trapped in buildings following natural disasters.

- Dogs are also being used in schools to improve children's behaviour, and trials are taking place with dogs that might be able to 'sniff out' the first signs of illness in some people.

- The 'pat a pet' service is a scheme where patients' pets are taken into hospital to help their owners to recover from illness.

DID YOU KNOW?

Over 1000 hearing dogs are now working throughout England, Scotland, Wales and Northern Ireland to help deaf people live better lives. Dogs are trained to alert deaf people to specific sounds, whether in the home, workplace or public buildings.

INDIRECT ANIMAL AND WILDLIFE OCCUPATIONS

The final category deals with jobs that have a clear link to animals, but are somewhat removed from those listed above. Into this category fall examples such as animal nutrition experts, who design special menus for sick animals or those that require specific diets. People working in shops such as tack shops or feed merchants also work in indirect animal occupations. There are also various education-related jobs that fall into this category, such as teaching people about animal conservation in college or university.

SUMMARY

The summary table on pages 30–2 highlights key information about the range of jobs available working with animals and wildlife. For each category of job, there is a specific example given to illustrate the qualifications required, skills/attributes needed and likely starting salaries. Enthusiasm, commitment and lots of initiative are needed for all jobs working with animals and wildlife.

FINDING OUT MORE

When you are ready to carry out more research about a specific job, get in touch with employers. Many provide very helpful information packs that give much more specific detail about what the jobs are like than is possible here. Websites are also a key source of up-to-date information, with useful ones listed in the resources section at the end of this book.

Category of job	Examples	Specific example	Relevant qualifications (highest level listed)	Skills/ attributes needed	Approximate annual starting salary
Animal health and welfare	veterinary work, physiotherapist, animal behaviourist, dog warden, alternative therapist, animal technician	Veterinary nurse *Note: minimum age for enrolment 17*	4/5 GCSEs at A*–C including English language, maths and a physical or biological science	Interpersonal skills, communication skills, empathy, ability to work in a team	£9000
Animal care charities	rescue centres worker, charity jobs	RSPCA inspector *Note: minimum age for enrolment 22*	GCSEs in English language and science	Compassion for animals, confidence, communication skills, ability to manage confrontation	£16,000

Sector	Jobs	Example	Qualifications	Skills	Salary
Wildlife management and conservation	scientific researcher, gamekeeper, ecologist, farm wildlife adviser, marine biologist	Biodiversity officer	Degree in ecology or environmental science or related area	Field identification skills, computer skills, communication skills, report writing skills, influencing skills, data management skills	£18,000
The animal and wildlife business	farmer, fish farmer, auctioneer, work with race-horses, riding instructor, horse stud, river bailiff, animal breeder or trainer, kennels and cattery worker, zoos, falconer, wildlife entertainment and tourism	Zookeeper	No specific qualifications needed (on-the-job training provided), but many applicants have done animal care courses	Respect for animals, good communication skills, physical fitness	£10,000

Category of job	Examples	Specific example	Relevant qualifications (highest level listed)	Skills/attributes needed	Approximate annual starting salary
Services provided through animals	dog handler for police or customs, mounted police	Dog handler	No specific qualifications needed (on-the-job training provided), but many applicants have done animal care courses	Affinity with animals, communication skills, confidence	£12,000
Indirect animal occupations	animal nutrition, working in a pet food shop, tack shop or feed merchants, education	Tack shop owner	No specific qualifications needed, but good business sense is important	Business and enterprise skills, communication skills, specialist knowledge of subject	Depends on success of business – sometimes very little on start up

5

Real lives 2

FLORUS OSKAM – VET

Veterinary science is one of the most sought-after of professions, with thousands of young people competing each year for the university places on offer. But what is daily life really like for a vet, and does it live up to the reputation it has gained from the media? To answer these questions we interviewed Florus Oskam, who works as a vet with the Dalehead Veterinary Group in Settle, North Yorkshire. He works mainly with horses.

What's a typical day like?
'There's no such thing as a typical day when you're a vet! Today my day started at 8.00am at the surgery, where I stopped to check what visits there were to do. Then I went to the equine therapy centre where the 'in-patients' were waiting for me. Depending on which horses are in and what their needs are, the work ranges from changing dressings to administering drugs. After this, on some days there are operations to do, and on other days I have to visit people's homes or carry out lameness work and X-rays. Breaks and lunchtimes are never guaranteed and some days there may not be time for any.

Get going – if you want to do well you need to get stuck in as soon as possible.

My day finishes at about 6.30pm. In winter this is often earlier as there isn't much scanning and reproduction work and people get their horses in earlier.'

There's no such thing as a typical day when you're a vet!

When did you decide you wanted to be a vet?
'I was born on a farm and always wanted to be a vet, working with horses in particular. I never considered any other career.'

What personal qualities do you think are important for this job?
'Dedication is probably the main one, and motivation. Working as a vet is not your typical nine-to-five job – it's a way of life. You do need to be academic to be able to train as a vet, but when it comes down to it, dedication is the most important personal quality.'

What are the advantages and disadvantages of working as a vet?
'It enables you to be a free person: you don't have anyone standing over you watching what you are doing all the time. It's also nice that no two days are the same – you never know what the day is going to bring. The disadvantage of the job is the social side of things. Making appointments to go out with friends is very difficult because you can never tell what time you'll be able to finish.'

What are your plans for the future?
'I want to become better at what I'm doing. There are further certificates that you can do and I would like to do some of these.'

KAYLEIGH McINTYRE – TRAINEE VETERINARY NURSE

For those interested in a career within a vets' practice, then it is not a lost cause if you're not academic enough to get the grades to become a vet. Veterinary nursing is an alternative career route to consider, and it is now possible to study this subject to degree level at university. To find out more about this important role, we interviewed Kayleigh McIntyre, who is a trainee veterinary nurse at the Dalehead Veterinary Group where Florus (see above) works as a vet.

What's a typical day like?
'A rota is done each week so what we do on the various days is decided beforehand. The days include:

- Kennel days
- 'Admits' (admit and discharge for operations) and puppy and kitten clinics
- 'Op days', where the nurses assist with surgical procedures and X-rays
- 'Lates' which are days when we have to stay for evening surgery which finishes at 7.00pm.

'Today is a kennel day, starting at 8.00am. The first half-hour is spent cleaning kennels, giving medication, checking drips, feeding and then writing up each dog's records. From 8.30am until 9.00am we do the kennel rounds where every 'in-patient' is discussed – what has to be done with them, whether they're going home or not, etc.

'At 9.00am the veterinary nurse on admit brings through the animals that are having operations and our job is to weigh them. This morning I assisted with a dog dental that involved extracting some teeth and a clean and polish. Nurses can clean and polish, but aren't able to do any other procedures.

'Next there was a dog with a wound that had to be re-sutured. 'Suturing' is the technical name for stitching a wound. Some more serious wounds need these stitches to be replaced every so often, or occasionally stitches drop out, and the stitches are put in again in a process known as 're-suturing'. After the re-suturing, we gave a rabbit a tear duct flush. Lunchtimes vary, as they are staggered between the nurses working to ensure that there's a nurse supervising animals recovering from anaesthetics at all times.

'In the afternoon the kennels are swept and mopped, drips are checked and the dogs are fed. I then do any lab work that needs doing, which could include running through samples or doing urine tests. Finally any animals that need discharging are discharged and I ensure that all relevant owners have been telephoned.

'Finishing times are variable from 4.30pm onwards, but they're not guaranteed. Sometimes I work overtime if, for example, an emergency comes in.'

When did you first become interested in animals?
'At the age of 3.'

When did you decide to do veterinary nursing?
'When I left school after doing my GCSEs.'

Did you consider any other jobs?
'Yes, I did consider doing equine physiotherapy and I would
like to have been a vet if I had got the grades.'

What training have you had?
'At the moment I'm doing a pre-vet nursing course (which is
designed for people who don't have the appropriate
GCSEs), and to do this you need to be a working at a vets'
practice. I've also done a National Diploma in Animal Care.'

Is the work what you expected it to be?
'Yes – and more.'

What hours do you do in a typical week?
'32 hours plus overtime (which I can either be paid for or
take as time off in lieu).'

What plans do you have for the future?
'I hope to become a fully qualified small animal nurse and
fully qualified equine veterinary nurse.'

Work hard and show that you can apply
yourself to any situation.

What are the highs and lows of the job?
'The highs of the job are working with very ill animals and
seeing them go home 100% recovered, especially when you
haven't expected them to survive. The lows of the job are
when animals come in that have to be put to sleep.'

Do salary levels reflect the work that you have to do?
'Not at all.'

*What advice would you give someone interested in pursuing
a career in this field?*
'The best thing that you can do is to get as much work
experience as possible, and try to get any work placements
you do at a veterinary surgery. Work hard and show that you
can apply yourself to any situation.

GAVIN CLUNIE – ANIMAL CARER

*Looking after animals in a zoo or safari park often comes
high on the wish list of people wanting to work in this area.
Gavin Clunie, who features in the next interview, works as an
animal carer in the rhino section at the South Lakes Wild
Animal Park in Dalton-in-Furness. He has worked there for
approximately two years, but prior to this worked as a crisis
journalist in war-torn countries.*

What's a typical day like?
'I start my day at 8.00am. On arrival at work the first stop is
the 'brew room' where we have a cup of tea or coffee and a
quick chat to share information with other members of staff
about the current happenings around the park. I then check
every single animal (at present I work in the rhino section but
I also care for the giraffes, baboons and porcupines).
Mucking out is the next job and this involves a big dumper
truck! I also make sure that the areas where the public walk
are clean and that the information boards and signs are
correct and ready for the visitors.

'At 10.00am we have a keepers' meeting for about half an
hour (including another brew). During this time, I fill in the

welfare diary, where we write information on the animals – for example noting details of mating cycles. This diary ensures that every keeper is aware of all the welfare issues.

'When the meeting has finished any jobs still to do are completed and then I prepare food for the animals in my section. Our lunch break is next and can be anywhere between five minutes and half an hour – the time is not guaranteed, as the animals do not work to a timetable!

'Next job is the hay run and there can be up to 60 bales of hay to move. I then check that all the equipment is clean and ready for the next day. Planning ahead is important to ensure smooth running from day to day.

'Then I have another brew before doing the giraffe talk for the public. Giraffes eat leaves in the boughs of trees, so after the talk I cut some off the trees around the park, and prepare breakfast for the other animals in my section ready for the morning.

'Finally I go and get the animals in. This job can take five minutes or two hours. If it has been raining the rhinos love the mud pool in the bottom of the field, and are somewhat reluctant to come in! My day ends at 5.30pm or 7.30pm. I

Our lunch break can be anywhere between five minutes and half an hour – the time is not guaranteed, as the animals do not work to a timetable!

do work long hours in the summer, but in the winter when there aren't as many visitors I get some 'time back'. This is not a nine-to-five job.'

When did you first become interested in working with animals?
'Previously I was a crisis journalist, and had no interest in zoo jobs. However, I had some experience of animals through my family, from having animals around. I got this job because I broke my ankle in a skiing accident and, while I was recuperating, I sent a few CVs out. I was asked to an interview at the park, and subsequently got this job. Looking back, I realise that I must have had some key transferable skills from my previous jobs that gave me an advantage over other applicants.'

What are the highs and lows of the job?
'The lows of the job are always stinking of you know what! And it's hard work physically. The highs of the job are that it's so wonderful to be surrounded by so many different animals every day.'

What training did you do?
'The training was on the job. To begin with I shadowed other keepers for a week. Over the next 12 weeks I started to do things on my own. Some people who work here have animal management degrees, but the most important things are that you use common sense, are assertive and are prepared to work.'

What personal qualities do you think are important for the job?
'You need to be outgoing and confident. I also have to do

talks and am surrounded by the general public, so tolerance is a useful quality. The rest you learn as you're going along.'

JENNY HOLDEN – OWL CHARITY CONSERVATION OFFICER

Some people's ambition is to work with wild animals rather than those in captivity. This is a dream that has been realised by Jenny Holden, who is a conservation officer for the World Owl Trust based at Muncaster Castle, Cumbria. In this interview she tells us more about her role.

What's a typical day like?
'Normally I start work at 8.00am, but today it was 6.00am, because, at the moment, I'm hand-rearing a badger and two owls. On the way to work, I checked two barn owl nest sites and found that in one of the nests the eggs had hatched. Whilst I was at the sites I also collected some owl pellets.

'At 9.30am I arrived at work and the day started with a group of school students. They met the owls and I did some pellet dissection with them. Next on the day's job list was checking letters and emails. We liaise with various other conservation organisations and government departments such as the Department for Environment, Food and Rural Affairs (DEFRA). I regularly attend shows with the birds to give talks, so I spent some time planning these.

'Careful records are kept of all the nest sites in order to keep a check on the owl populations to see whether they are increasing or declining. After planning the talks, I continued to write up some of the results from last year. The records are computerised so, after visiting the nest sites, I enter the data into the computer, including details like the number of chicks and eggs. If we can catch the parents, we put rings on their legs with identification numbers so they can be traced.

'After this, I spent some time with the birds we use for the educational visits – Jimmy the eagle owl and Mia the short-eared owl. At 4.00pm I started to prepare for the Crick Boat Show this coming weekend, where I will be giving a couple of talks. Today my day will not finish until about 9.00pm because, when I leave work, I am going to a meeting with local farmers and DEFRA.'

When did you first become interested in animals?
'When I was 3 – I used to crawl around the garden picking up creepy crawlies! From the age of 7 I'd go out on to the wildlife reserves and, at age 11, I worked with a hill sheep farmer. When I was 14, I did my first zoo work experience and continued in this field working at Chester Zoo and, while at university, at London Zoo.'

What animals do you work with?
'I do a lot of work with owls, which are the top predators in the food chain. But I look at the whole food chain, so this includes butterfly and red squirrel conservation. I'm a licensed bat worker and do this in my spare time.'

Did you consider any other jobs?
'Not really, I always wanted to do this.'

What hours do you work in an average week?
'Officially 40 hours – unofficially, unlimited hours. I always have a tent in my car so that I can camp next to owl nest

sites. I try to catch up on hours in the winter time when it
tends to be quieter.'

What training do you have?
'I have a BSc in Biology and Media. I write for magazines
and newspapers to supplement my income. I'm a licensed
bird ringer as well as a bat worker.'

*What advice would you give somebody interested in
pursuing a career in this field?*
'Get going – if you want to do well you need to get stuck in
as soon as possible. The more you do with different species
of animal the better. Wildlife Watch is a good group to join
(it's the junior arm of the wildlife trusts) as they give you the
chance to meet reserve wardens, which helps you to make
contacts. Some of the major zoos such as Chester Zoo have
placement schemes for older students, which allow you to
work with a keeper for a month. You need to gain as much
experience as possible. There are hundreds of graduates out
there and you need to stand out from the rest.'

Wading through piles of smelly owl pellets is not
much fun until you find something interesting
like a bat skull ... then it's brilliant!

What are the highs and lows of the job?
'The highs have to be the close encounters with wild animals
or the discovery of a new nest site. I also find it very
interesting when I find a pattern in the data. The lows would
be having five school visits a week and answering the same
questions over and over. Wading through piles of smelly owl

pellets is not much fun until you find something interesting like a bat skull ... then it's brilliant!'

What plans do you have for the future?
'To start a PhD, then maybe move on to something more research-based. At the moment I'm happy to stay here and see the Owl Trust go forward. I may eventually go into broadcasting.'

6

Tools of the trade

Many young people have a romantic notion that working with animals is exotic and glamorous. Some think that the work only takes place in picturesque locations, where the weather is glorious. But reading through the stories of people already working in this field should balance this image. Whilst there are definitely plenty of positives, there are inevitably some negatives too and these represent key challenges for anybody considering working in this sector.

This chapter considers what you will need to make a success of a career working with animals and wildlife. The range of jobs you can do is bewildering, so the particular skills you might need for the career you choose could be quite specific. Nevertheless, it is possible to summarise some of the main skills and qualities you will need whatever job you find in this sector.

- Spending all day working with animals can be physically and mentally exhausting. A degree of **determination, stamina** and **patience** is, therefore, essential for working in this sector.
- You need to have total **dedication** to your work because you may have to work long and sometimes unsociable hours, with very little time off and minimum

pay. These are not the kind of jobs people do 'just for the money'.

- It is very rarely a nine-to-five, Monday-to-Friday job. Sometimes you could be required to work evenings and weekends, so Saturday nights out are never guaranteed. Therefore **flexibility** is obligatory. But if you have a **passion** for what you're doing you can feel a great sense of achievement when things work out well.

- Good levels of **physical fitness** and **endurance** are required, particularly if you're working on a stable yard or at an animal park and have to muck out ten animals a day! After a week of this even the physically fit will be tired.

- Most jobs will involve working with both animals and the public so good **communication skills** are essential. Take, for example, a veterinary practice where communication between the general public and members of your team would be a daily occurrence.

- **Teamwork** is very frequently required, so you should be able to work effectively as part of a team as well as on your own. Knowing when to take the lead and when others need to take charge is important, as is identifying what you need to do to help your team achieve its goals.

- Animal behaviour is unpredictable so you have to demonstrate **confidence** and show who is boss. The odd bite or kick could still occur; this is something you will need to get used to!

- A strong but **unsentimental commitment** to animals is crucial because, quite frequently, upsetting situations do arise when an animal might die. You sometimes have to make difficult decisions that are in the interests of the animal rather than designed to make you feel better.

- **Respect** and **compassion** for animals are important attributes as you'll be working with them on a daily basis. Remember that you are not going to be working with animals as pets, so you will need to develop a **professional** and **responsible attitude** to dealing with them.
- It is important **not to be squeamish** about animals' bodily functions or the sight of blood: if you are, then you will have to face up to these issues pretty soon if you are serious about working with animals or wildlife.

Some jobs are quite academic; others require practical skills while others need you to have a good business sense. It is therefore important to be clear about what particular skills and qualities are important in the job(s) you are most interested in. To do this you should talk to people already carrying out the job. Listen carefully to what they have to say and try to imagine yourself in the job on a day-to-day basis. If you start to have second thoughts then you might want to reconsider whether the job really is for you!

Quiz

This quiz is intended to help you find out how much you know about animals and wildlife. It will also allow you to consider some of the key issues about working in this sector.

WHAT DO YOU KNOW ABOUT WORKING WITH ANIMALS?

Read the questions overleaf and decide which are the correct answers. Note that some questions have more than one correct answer.

1 WWF stands for ...

   A Wildlife and Wilderness Fund
   B World Wildlife Fund
   C World Whale Fund

2 If you were a farrier, what job would you be doing?

   A Fitting saddles
   B Shoeing horses
   C Training horses

3 An aviary is ...

   A A place where bees live
   B A duck's nest
   C A large cage or building where birds are kept

4 What does RSPB stand for?

   A Royal Society for the Protection of Birds
   B Royal Service for Protecting Birds
   C Royal Society for the Protection of Bats

5 Which of the following are breeds of dog?

   A Newfoundland
   B Persian
   C Labradoodle

6 A gelding is ...

   A A castrated male horse
   B Any castrated male
   C A castrated male dog

7 A National Nature Reserve is ...

   A A site that protects an area of historic interest

    B A government-designated area of national importance for wildlife or geology

    C A site where rare animals are bred

8 A cattery is ...

    A A place where cats are treated

    B A place where cats are groomed

    C A place where cats are bred or looked after

9 What does RSPCA stand for?

    A Royal Society for the Prevention of Cruelty to Animals

    B Royal Society for the Protection and Care of Animals

    C Royal Society for the Prevention of Cruelty to Antelopes

10 What does an ecologist do?

    A Studies snakes in captivity

    B Examines the relationship between the environment and actions that affect it

    C Works out the budget for wildlife areas

11 Which of the following is the UK nationally important for?

    A Breeding seabirds

    B Flamingos on migration

    C Wintering wading birds and ducks

ANSWERS

1 **B**. The WWF (World Wildlife Fund) was launched officially on 11 September 1961. It is now a truly global conservation organisation that has been instrumental in making the environment a matter of world concern. In some parts of the world the WWF is also known as the World Wide Fund for Nature.

2 **B**. A farrier is someone who shoes horses. A farrier is a skilled craftsperson who has a good knowledge of the theory and practice of horse shoeing.

3 **C**. An aviary is a large cage or building where birds are kept. Aviaries are used to keep birds in zoos, and in people's homes where birds are kept as pets.

4 **A**. The RSPB (Royal Society for the Protection of Birds) has been working with wild birds and conservation since 1889. The work of the RSPB is carried out throughout the UK, helping to conserve and safeguard the future of birds. Amongst the many tasks carried out by the RSPB are developing and managing over 100 nature reserves across the UK and carrying out research work to help understand why certain birds are on the decline and how they can be brought back from the brink of extinction.

5 **A** (Newfoundland) and **C** (Labradoodle) are both breeds of dog. The Labradoodle was originally a cross between a Labrador Retriever and a Standard Poodle, but it is now a breed all of its own. The Persian is a breed of cat.

6 **A**. A gelding is a castrated male horse. Castration or gelding is the removal of the horse's testicles. This operation is carried out to make the horse more placid, in particular when in the company of mares (females), and to sterilise it. The most popular age for gelding a horse is between one and two years.

7 **B**. National Nature Reserves (NNRs) were established to protect the most important areas of wildlife habitat and geological formations in the UK, and as places for scientific

research. They are owned by the government nature conservation agency English Nature or private land owners, and managed by English Nature or approved bodies such as the wildlife trusts.

8 **C**. A cattery is a place where cats are bred or looked after. People often take their cats to a cattery for safe keeping when they go on holiday.

9 **A**. The RSPCA was launched in 1824, and was originally known as the SPCA (Society for the Prevention of Cruelty to Animals). It was not until 1840 that the name changed to The Royal Society for the Prevention of Cruelty to Animals when Queen Victoria gave her permission for it to be changed.

10 **B**. Ecologists are employed in a variety of organisations to carry out research or ensure that wildlife is protected. Actions that can affect the environment include rainfall, farming, pollution, temperature shifts and industrialisation.

11 **A** and **C**. The UK has huge populations of breeding seabirds on its cliffs and in the winter our estuaries are teeming with waders and wildfowl from Russia and Scandinavia, which find food in abundance. The nearest wild flamingos live in France.

Now add up your score, and have a look at the box overleaf to see how you did.

- 0–3 answers correct: hard luck – read this book to find out more!
- 4–6 answers correct: not bad – but you should widen your knowledge.
- 7–9 answers correct: well done – you have good knowledge of this field.
- 10–11 answers correct: you're a superstar!

Don't worry if your score wasn't perfect – there's lots to learn in any profession.

Challenges to consider

Working with animals and wildlife can be one of the most satisfying of jobs, but it can also be one of the most challenging. This chapter considers the challenges it poses, which you need to bear in mind when considering working in this sector. If you haven't really thought deeply about what working in this sector would be like on a day-to-day basis, this chapter might serve as a wake-up call for you.

LONG AND UNSOCIABLE HOURS

As you will have seen from the Case studies and Real lives chapters in this book, those people who work with animals and wildlife often mention the unsociable hours that accompany the job. As animals are not very good at keeping to diary schedules, you should expect to work erratic hours, often getting up at the crack of dawn or staying late into the evening.

This makes it difficult to have a normal social life, and means that your friends and loved ones need to be really understanding of your situation. Unfortunately, these long hours are not necessarily reflected in the pay you receive, and overtime pay is not always provided. Instead, a flexible view is often taken, and you're expected to 'catch up' with your private time when things are less busy.

Real-life story: surveying the jungle

'I once spent three months living in a tent carrying out surveys of rainforest wildlife in Ecuador, South America. It was one of the most amazing times of my life, but it was really tough too. We ate sardines and rice every night for the first month, and found it hard to get hold of water that was clean enough to drink.

We found ourselves on the menu for the hordes of mosquitoes and other biting insects that buzzed around us in clouds. The insects were so bad that we had to use a special repellent spray that contained such powerful chemicals that it stripped the outer layer off our skin! For a toilet we dug a hole in the ground, and the only place to wash properly was in a nearby river, where piranha fish lurked.

Arriving direct from a comfortable lifestyle back home, where every modern convenience was at our fingertips, we soon learned that we were going to have to adapt quickly if we were to enjoy our stay in the jungle.

Brin Best

HOSTILE WORKING CONDITIONS

You will undoubtedly need to be a hardy soul to put up with the tough working conditions associated with many jobs working with animals and wildlife. If you are somebody who hates getting cold and wet or hot and sweaty, then this is probably not a career for you.

Likewise, you may well encounter mud, blood, urine and animal dung at some point during your working week, so if you're squeamish about these things you will need to develop a tougher attitude pretty soon if you're going to survive!

Many jobs working in this sector also require you to work outside, often in remote, hostile locations for lengthy periods of time. Although it is unlikely that you will be asked to work alone in the wilderness, having a strong independent streak will be a distinct advantage.

HEALTH AND SAFETY ISSUES
Working with animals and wildlife has its fair share of health and safety risks. While it is not as dangerous as some professions (such as the armed forces), you should be aware that cuts, bruises and occasionally more serious incidents will happen from time to time.

Animals can be unpredictable and you should not take it personally if they bite or kick you occasionally. For this reason you are not likely to enjoy working in this sector if you are fussy about getting the odd splinter, cut or bruise.

Bear in mind also that you will need a good level of physical fitness for many jobs working with animals and wildlife. A

Animals can be unpredictable and you should not take it personally if they bite or kick you occasionally.

Real-life story: a pleasant summer ride ...

It was a beautiful sunny summer's day and my friend and I were riding our horses to get them fit for a competition. The bridleway that we had chosen took us near a river. It was a flat, open space alongside the river so we were cantering along when my horse got spooked by a distant object. Her whole body tensed and despite my efforts to keep her going forwards, she was determined to do the opposite. I could sense the river getting closer and I knew the steep, grassy banks could give way at any moment. The next thing I knew we were in the river, by which point we had parted company! The adrenalin kicked in and all I could think about was getting her out. She was thrashing about in the water, which was deep, and as I struggled to grab the reins she launched herself over the top of me in a bid to get out. Amazingly she managed to scramble onto the riverbank, but cut herself badly. Needless to say we had to call the vet, but astoundingly we both escaped with only cuts and bruises.

Felicity Haynes

certain amount of basic strength will come in useful if you're handling animals, especially the larger ones.

EMOTIONAL ENGAGEMENT

There is no getting away from the fact that working with animals and wildlife can be emotionally draining. Despite trying to maintain a professional attitude to your work, it is easy to get attached to animals and it is sometimes necessary to make difficult life and death decisions that are hard to come to terms with.

This presents a key challenge for anyone considering working in this field. Although over time you will become more accustomed to making these difficult decisions, it will never be easy.

Real-life story: a difficult decision

A call came in to the sanctuary to say that an injured fox had been found on the side of the road. I dashed to the site to discover a young vixen hiding in the bushes with what appeared to be two broken legs. She was having difficulty moving, so we managed to catch her in a large net. We took her straight back to the sanctuary where a vet came to look at her. She was a beautiful animal, with sleek fur and a big bushy tail. The vet looked worried as he was examining the fox and she howled in pain as he touched her back. He shook his head and said that this poor animal was beyond help, as she had broken bones in her back. The kindest thing was to put her to sleep. I found it difficult to settle that night thinking about what we might have done to save her life if we'd arrived earlier, but I now realise we did all that we could.

Jarvis Hayes

Training day

8

One thing is certain about a career working with animals and wildlife – there is no single entry route in terms of qualifications and training. The range of professions is so wide: some require study to degree or even postgraduate level; others allow you to train on the job, having obtained a basic school education. A few don't even ask for any qualifications, just a willingness to learn new skills as you work.

ASK YOURSELF SOME KEY QUESTIONS
Before beginning to think about the different training routes for specific jobs, it is a good idea to sit down and have a long think about some basic questions:

- What qualifications are you currently studying for?
- What choices await you in terms of the qualifications that you can take?
- Are you the kind of person who prefers hands-on training on the job or studying at school, college or university?
- Do you have what it takes to get the grades needed to go to college or university to follow a specific course?
- Would you have the staying power to stick at a three- or five-year training course?
- Do you like courses that are focused on a particular job (vocational) or those that provide a broader education (academic)?
- Are you happy to take on the financial strain of studying full time? Many students leave college or university with large debts (£13,000 is not unusual).

In answering these questions you might like to talk things through with another person, for example one of your parents, a friend or a teacher. Whoever you do it with, it is vital to be totally honest about your capabilities and personal qualities. While there is no doubt that hard work and determination count for a lot, there is no use being unrealistic about what you can achieve academically.

Tens of thousands of young people considering a career working with animals and wildlife have their hearts set on becoming a vet, yet the number of students who graduate each year with a degree in veterinary science from UK universities is relatively small, with only a handful of universities offering courses. Competition for places is fierce, and you have to get very high grades at A level just to stand a chance of being offered a place on a course.

THE DIFFERENT PATHWAYS

The flowchart on the next page outlines a number of pathways into a career working with animals and wildlife. Because of the broad range of jobs available, you are sure to find a route that suits you. There are alternative routes that are worth bearing in mind too.

Many people study at university as 'mature students' (aged 21 or over), often on a part-time basis while working. It is perfectly possible to mix and match these qualifications at different times during your career. Your progression through your career is also likely to be marked by on-the-job qualifications and training at different levels, according to your particular interests and work demands.

access to careers

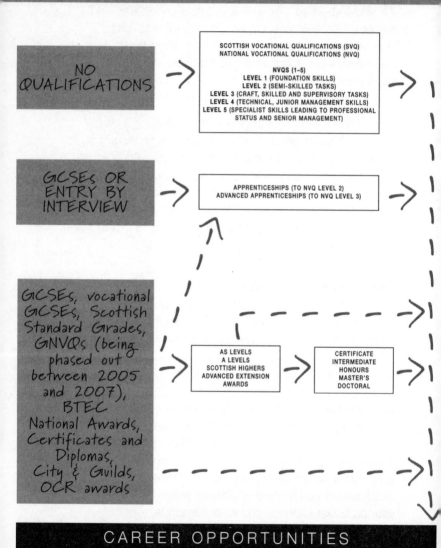

NO QUALIFICATIONS

SCOTTISH VOCATIONAL QUALIFICATIONS (SVQ)
NATIONAL VOCATIONAL QUALIFICATIONS (NVQ)

NVQS (1–5)
LEVEL 1 (FOUNDATION SKILLS)
LEVEL 2 (SEMI-SKILLED TASKS)
LEVEL 3 (CRAFT, SKILLED AND SUPERVISORY TASKS)
LEVEL 4 (TECHNICAL, JUNIOR MANAGEMENT SKILLS)
LEVEL 5 (SPECIALIST SKILLS LEADING TO PROFESSIONAL STATUS AND SENIOR MANAGEMENT)

GCSEs OR ENTRY BY INTERVIEW

APPRENTICESHIPS (TO NVQ LEVEL 2)
ADVANCED APPRENTICESHIPS (TO NVQ LEVEL 3)

GCSEs, vocational GCSEs, Scottish Standard Grades, GNVQs (being phased out between 2005 and 2007), BTEC National Awards, Certificates and Diplomas, City & Guilds, OCR awards

AS LEVELS
A LEVELS
SCOTTISH HIGHERS
ADVANCED EXTENSION AWARDS

CERTIFICATE
INTERMEDIATE
HONOURS
MASTER'S
DOCTORAL

CAREER OPPORTUNITIES

NOTE: Mature students (aged 21 or over) often do not have to obtain as high examination grades as those going straight from school to universit

These qualifications all form part of a new National Qualifications Framework (see www.qca.org.uk), which has eight levels (see page 62).

APPRENTICESHIPS

There has been a large increase in the take-up of apprenticeships in recent years, and there are now over 180 to choose from across more than 80 industry sectors. Perhaps the reason why they have been so popular is that they provide you with the best of both worlds. They allow you to study for a nationally-recognised qualification and gain on-the-job training, while at the same time earning money. The fact that you gain valuable work experience is also a real bonus, since this is highly regarded by employers.

If you sign up for an apprenticeship you will need determination to succeed. You will have to commit yourself to at least one year of training and study, with some schemes asking you to sign up for two or even five years. You will also need to be able to switch from working one day to studying at college the next. A selection of apprenticeships linked to working with animals and wildlife is shown below, but note that new ones are being phased in all the time (visit www.apprenticeships.org.uk for more details):

- Agriculture, crops and livestock
- Animal care
- Environmental conservation
- Farriery
- The equine industry.

Apprenticeships are open-ended, allowing you to complete the course in your own time. Although they used to be

The National Qualifications Framework

Level	Example qualifications	Framework for Higher Education Qualifications	Example careers
1	GCSE grades D–G; NVQ level 1	n/a	Horse groom, zookeeper, feed merchant worker, kennel hand, dog warden
2	GCSE grades A*–C; NVQ level 2	n/a	RSPCA inspector, veterinary nurse, gamekeeper
3	A levels; NVQ level 3; BTEC diplomas, certificates and awards	n/a	Farmer, wildlife tourism officer, charity campaigner
4	NVQ level 4; BTEC Diplomas, Certificates and Awards	Certificate (certificates of further and higher education)	Animal technician, riding instructor, head zookeeper
5	NVQ level 4; BTEC Diplomas, Certificates and Awards	Intermediate (diplomas of higher education, foundation degrees, higher national diplomas)	Yard manager, park ranger, bird surveyor
6	NVQ level 4	Honours (bachelor's degrees, graduate certificates and diplomas)	Conservation scientist, vet, animal physiotherapist, animal behaviourist, ecologist, reserve warden, farm manager
7	NVQ level 5	Master's (master's degrees, postgraduate certificates and diplomas)	Marine biologist, specialist wildlife adviser, senior charity worker
8	NVQ level 5	Doctoral (doctorates)	Senior wildlife researcher, university lecturer

aimed at young people, there is now no age limit for who can apply. To be accepted onto an apprenticeship you may need GCSEs in certain subjects; this will be dependent on the apprenticeship. You may also have to take some sort of test before being accepted, or perhaps an interview.

To get on to an apprenticeship you can approach an employer directly or apply through the Learning and Skills Council (www.lsc.gov.uk). For apprenticeships available outside England visit www.scottish-enterprise.com (Scotland), www.elwa.ac.uk (Wales) and www.delni.gov.uk (Northern Ireland).

Remember that getting accepted is like being offered any new job, and employers will only take you on if they think you are right for the job.

GCSES AND A LEVELS

This is the traditional education route for most students in England, Wales and Northern Ireland, with Standard and Higher Grade equivalents in Scotland. In recent years vocational GCSEs have been introduced, which are qualifications linked to a specific job type. They are beginning to replace the General National Vocational Qualifications (GNVQs) which are now being phased out. The new Advanced Extension Awards (AEAs) allow study beyond A level standard for high-flyers.

NATIONAL VOCATIONAL QUALIFICATIONS

The appearance in recent years of National Vocational Qualifications (NVQs) at five levels has allowed people to obtain work-based qualifications while doing a job. NVQs are open to people of all ages and abilities, and relate directly to the job you are carrying out. Scotland has its own version – the Scottish Vocational Qualifications.

The five levels that can be obtained through NVQs are shown in the flow chart on page 60. The higher the number, the higher the level of specialisation and managerial duties you will be carrying out. NVQs are an indication of how well you carry out a particular task, and the knowledge and understanding you have to perform your job well. When working towards an NVQ you can be given credit for the skills you may have already gained through your experience carrying out a job.

BTEC NATIONAL QUALIFICATIONS

These are qualifications focusing on a specialist occupational area and leading into employment or higher education. There are three levels: Award, Certificate and Diploma, which are roughly equivalent to one, two or three A levels. BTEC diplomas are sometimes used as an alternative route of entry for students going to university. For further details check out www.edexcel.org.uk.

CITY & GUILDS

City & Guilds is a leading provider of vocational qualifications in the UK. Their qualifications assess skills that are of practical value in the workplace, with over 500 different qualifications to choose from. Jamie Oliver, Gary Rhodes and Alan Titchmarsh have all studied for City & Guilds qualifications earlier in their careers. City & Guilds are also closely linked with the apprenticeships scheme described earlier. Find out more at www.cityandguilds.com.

OCR AWARDS

OCR offers a wide range of qualifications, some of which provide an alternative route to the traditional GCSE and A levels taken by most students at school. These include Vocationally Related Certificates and OCR Nationals. Note that your local school/college will not offer all of the vast range of courses on offer. For more information visit www.ocr.org.uk.

OTHER CERTIFICATES AND DIPLOMAS

These qualifications, offered by colleges and some universities, take study to a higher level in a specific area. One of the most popular of these is the Higher National Diploma (HND), which allows study in an area that is closely related to a profession, such as countryside management or horse studies. These courses are usually at least one year in length, often two and sometimes even more if you study part time. You can study for an HND in a wide range of subject areas, and these courses are ideal if you are not sure whether you want to commit to a degree course. There is the option to convert to a degree later if you wish to go down this route.

DEGREE-LEVEL STUDY AND BEYOND

For some careers it is necessary to obtain degree-level qualifications. Most jobs that need a good scientific grasp of the subject matter fall into this category. Courses at this level now come in a wide range of types and levels, with the UCAS website being a goldmine of information on this education route (www.ucas.ac.uk). Traditionally the preserve of universities, degrees are now being offered by an increasing number of further education colleges too.

FOUNDATION DEGREES

These may suit people wanting to study at university level while continuing their working life. Employers are involved in the design of these courses in collaboration with colleges and universities. This means that the courses are often available locally. Flexible study methods (eg distance learning, evening classes) ease the burden on those in work. They take two to four years to complete, depending on whether you study full or part time. There is also the option to continue for another period to complete an honours degree. With no set entry requirements and account taken of any previous experience in a job, these degrees are becoming more and more popular.

HONOURS DEGREES

Honours degrees, such as Bachelor of Arts or Bachelor of Science, are the most common degrees offered. They take from three to five years full time depending on the course taken, and can also be taken part time or by flexible learning (or a mixture of the two). Many degrees are focused on a specific subject, rather than being pitched at a particular profession. As such they can offer a wide range of employment options if you are still undecided about a precise career.

MASTER'S DEGREES AND DOCTORATES

These qualifications, which are only offered by universities, are the pinnacle of academic study. Master's degrees usually take one year full time and typically combine a taught element with a research project. They focus on a very specific area of study, which is sometimes closely related to a profession (eg wildlife management, animal health and welfare). Doctorates are a major undertaking, requiring at least three years of full-time study. They are mostly research-based, requiring you to carry out in-depth studies on a topic of your choice and write a 100,000 word thesis on your findings. Many people who do doctorates stay on at university to continue their research, as well as lecturing students.

GENERAL ADVICE

Other advice that will help you to decide on appropriate entry routes for specific careers includes:

- Talk to people about what specific training courses or qualifications are like, but remember that they are giving *their* views and you might find things are different for you.
- Pay visits to colleges and universities to find out more about the courses and what student life is like there.
- Some courses offer sampler days that allow you to get a taste of the course without committing yourself.
- Read up about different training routes for specific careers, making sure you take advantage of websites, which often contain the most up-to-date information.
- Don't rush into any decisions; any course is a significant commitment and you need to be sure that you have made the right choice.

AMANDA BEST

Case study 2

9

BIODIVERSITY OFFICER
Amanda Best is a biodiversity officer for the Environment Agency, based in Leeds.

What's a typical day like?
'I start work in the office at about 8.30am and log on to catch up with any new emails. I will then typically have a range of reports or proposals to comment on to make sure that wildlife and nature conservation have been taken into account. An example would be a proposed new development next to a riverside. I would comment to make sure that buildings are set back from the riverbank, and that a 'green corridor' is kept along the river so that habitat is available for wildlife such as otters or kingfishers.

'I also spend time on my own projects to improve the environment for wildlife. This involves planning and developing project ideas, and working with other wildlife organisations to seek funding and deliver the work on the ground. The types of

The highs are knowing that you hav made an improvement to the environment that will be there for future generations t enjoy.

projects are wide-ranging, from carrying out surveys of protected species to creating large-scale new wetland habitats. Later in the day I may need to go out on site to assess impacts of a proposal in the field, or to a meeting to discuss projects or issues with other organisations.'

When did you first become interested in wildlife?
'I've been interested in wildlife since I was a child. I grew up on a farm and was surrounded by wildlife, and my mother particularly encouraged my interest in wild flowers.'

What species do you work with?
'I work mainly with those species that the Environment Agency is responsible for in the UK Biodiversity Action Plan, a national initiative to help threatened species and habitats. The main ones are the otter, water vole and white-clawed crayfish. These are by no means the only ones though, and work can include almost any UK native species given the wide-ranging work of the Environment Agency. However, it's generally those species associated with the aquatic environment.'

Did you consider any other jobs?
'Not really. I wasn't sure what I wanted to do but felt strongly that I wanted to do work that was linked to the outdoors and the countryside. I did apply for one or two jobs that were more linked to agriculture.'

What hours do you work in an average week?
'I work about 38 hours a week, but within a flexi-time system, so one week it can be more, the next fewer hours.'

What training do you have?
'I have a degree in ecology from the University of East
Anglia. The Environment Agency offers me training on

The lack of funding for nature conservation
work can often be very frustrating.

specific aspects of the job – this has included courses in
identifying plant species, how to manage projects, how to
influence people and in river restoration.

*What advice would you give somebody interested in
pursuing a career in this field?*
'Try to gain some experience and knowledge of wildlife and
natural history by joining a local wildlife group or by
volunteering for a local wildlife trust. Such groups usually
welcome new people and have much knowledge to share.
Wildlife trusts often need volunteers to help manage nature
reserves, and this can be a valuable way of learning about
the habitats and their management as well as the species
you may encounter. Many organisations such as the
Environment Agency will also offer work experience for a
couple of weeks to those who ask.'

What are the highs and lows of the job?
'The lack of funding for nature conservation work can often
be very frustrating. There's usually a long list of actions, with
no time or resources to spend on them. The highs though
are when you're able to see what you've achieved on the
ground – a new pond teeming with dragonflies, a new

meadow full of wild flowers, and knowing that you have made an improvement to the environment that will be there for future generations to enjoy.'

What plans do you have for the future?
'I plan to carry on working with wildlife into the future, hopefully delivering more large-scale habitat improvements.'

Getting a job

10

This chapter focuses on the mechanics of how to go about actually getting a job working with animals and wildlife. You will find some practical guidance about job hunting, making applications, compiling your CV and the interview process. There is also advice on climbing up the career ladder once you've landed your first job.

Before beginning your job search you should be clear about where you want to work in the country. Would you be happier staying near home or are you prepared to move to somewhere new? There might be some parts of the country that you would not consider for particular reasons. What about working overseas? Think this through at the start, but be aware that for some sought-after jobs you may have no choice over where you have to move.

FINDING APPROPRIATE JOBS

Doing your research when looking for a new job really pays dividends. Try to use as wide a range of different information sources as possible, including the following:

- The job centre
- Your local newspapers
- Specialist newspapers (eg the Wednesday edition of the *Guardian*)
- Magazines (eg *Farmers' Weekly*, *Fish Farmer*, *New Scientist*)

- Recruitment newsletters (eg *The Environment Post,* www.green4u.co.uk)
- Websites (eg www.lgjobs.com for local government vacancies)
- Any contacts you may already have in local organisations and companies.

The next step after finding a job that appears suitable is to do some preliminary research. This allows you to judge whether you should send in an application. You may also have to send off for an application form. Make sure you keep to the guidelines set out in the application pack (if there is one) or follow the application instructions outlined in the advert. Remember also to keep careful records of jobs you have applied for, with details of key dates such as when the interviews will take place.

YOUR CV

The term 'Curriculum Vitae' is derived from Latin and means literally 'course of life'. It is usually abbreviated to the more easily remembered 'CV'. Your CV is a way of selling yourself on one or two sides of A4 paper.

It summarises your qualifications, work experience, skills and interests and gives potential employers an overview of what you are like as a person. You are often required to send in your CV in response to job adverts, sometimes instead of filling in an application form.

A CV is a very important document. You should take a lot of care over producing it and make sure you use positive, persuasive and professional language. Never make things up on your CV; this could get you into serious hot water at interview and may even cost you your job if it turns out you misled your employer. Check everything really carefully, as spelling and grammar mistakes create a very bad impression. It is a good idea to get someone else to read over it to check it for errors.

This book is not the place to go into detail about compiling your CV; there are many other books on the topic and plenty of people out there that can help you. In particular, get the advice of a careers officer (via your school or college), who will be able to provide you with some useful guidance to help you make a professional job of your CV.

If you are asked to send in a CV you will probably also be asked to put a letter of application in with it. The purpose of this letter is for you to outline how your qualifications and experience meet the requirements of the job. As with your CV, it is a very important document and should be prepared very carefully.

APPLYING FOR JOBS

The application process for jobs usually follows a predictable pattern:

- The employer advertises the job in the press or job centre
- Applicants do some research to find out if they are interested in the job, and may need to contact the employer to request an application pack
- Applicants apply on an application form or send in their CV and a covering letter
- The employers draw up a shortlist of suitable applicants for interview

- The interviews take place and the final successful candidate is selected.

Many employers send out a standard application form, which you need to fill in as carefully as you would prepare your CV. To stand a better chance of being shortlisted for an interview it is important to try to stand out from the crowd by drawing attention to all your positive features.

INTERVIEWS

Like it or not, interviews are a standard hurdle to get over when trying to land a new job. Most people dislike interviews; they can be nerve-racking and it is tough being asked a whole raft of questions under pressure. But if you have managed to get an interview then you're a long way towards being offered a job, so it's well worth making a big effort. Some people find it helpful to carry out a mock interview with a friend or family member before the real thing.

When undertaking interviews make sure you:

- Research the employer and the job so you appear knowledgeable
- Remind yourself what you put in your application form/CV
- Dress smartly but don't go over the top with what you wear
- Smile a lot and make eye contact
- Appear positive and upbeat (nobody wants to employ someone who is miserable!)
- Prepare responses to some commonly-asked questions (eg Why did you apply for this job? What skills do you have that make you suitable?)

- Are honest and don't exaggerate your skills or abilities
- Are natural and yourself; don't pretend to be someone you're not
- Ask politely for a question to be repeated if you cannot answer it; this will give you some thinking time
- Are clear what the job is really like; ask questions if this needs clarification.

You should know if you have been successful in the interview either on the day itself or in the next couple of days. Employers telephone or write to all those interviewed to let them know the outcome. Sometimes a 'debrief' is offered if you are not successful. This gives the employer the chance to explain how you got on in the interview and why you didn't get the job. This kind of information is very helpful in planning for future interviews.

CLIMBING UP THE CAREER LADDER

It is likely that at some point in your career there will be opportunities to progress higher up in the organisation or company. This will allow you access to more responsibility, in return for a higher salary. But because it could also mean longer hours and more pressure, career progression isn't for everyone. Some people are quite happy to stay working at their current level; they feel comfortable there and enjoy the work.

DR PIRAN WHITE

Case study 3

11

UNIVERSITY ECOLOGY LECTURER

Dr Piran White is an ecology lecturer at York University, specialising in the ecology of mammals.

What's a typical day like?
'My time is officially divided up into 40% research, 30% teaching and 30% administration. There is no typical day; a day may be made up of all three, or just one of these activities. Research could mean doing some work in the field, for example tagging or radio-tracking animals, analysing some data, writing a scientific paper, discussing research plans and progress with a researcher or PhD student or writing a research proposal. Administration could involve working on student admissions or revising the structure of a degree programme. I teach courses in wildlife management both to undergraduates and to graduates, and I also run a field-based course for first year students.'

When did you first become interested in wildlife?
'My interest was first developed by watching birds feeding in my parents' garden and also by childhood trips to the

I'm involved in projects on possums in New Zealand and rabbits in Australia.

Natural History Museum in London, especially the dinosaur exhibits. As a child, I also enjoyed identifying butterflies and moths and looking after caterpillars.'

What species do you work with?
'My research involves a wide range of species. I work a lot with mammals including badgers, deer, foxes, hares and rabbits. My research on these species focuses on animal behaviour and how this is linked to the spread of disease, on how people interact with animals and on conservation. Some of this is done abroad, and I'm involved in projects on possums in New Zealand and rabbits in Australia.'

Did you consider other jobs?
'Before leaving school, I considered being a vet, a geologist and an archaeologist. Towards the end of my PhD, I also considered working in scientific publishing. After my postdoctoral research, I was offered a job as a research scientist in Denmark, but declined it, and the job at York came up soon afterwards.'

What hours do you work in an average week?
'40 hours.'

What training do you have?
'I have a BSc in ecology and a PhD. My PhD was on the behaviour of urban foxes and the implications for the spread of rabies.

What advice would you give somebody interested in pursuing a similar career?
'Opportunities for lectureships in ecology and wildlife management are relatively limited. It's common to need three

to five years of research experience, in addition to having a PhD. One of the most important factors that will help your chances of reaching the interview stage is having a good record of scientific publications in international journals. Although only 40% of your time is spent doing research, it's your research rather than your abilities in teaching or administration that mainly determines your promotion prospects. At the newer universities, you may spend a much greater proportion of your time teaching, with much less time available for research.'

It's your research rather than your abilities in teaching or administration that mainly determines your promotion prospects.

What are the highs and lows of the job?
'One of the greatest benefits of the job is being able to spend time working on things that interest you and also the feeling that what you're doing can make a real difference to wildlife conservation and management. For example, I've been involved in research that's contributed directly to the debates on hunting with dogs and bovine tuberculosis.

'The job is also quite flexible. To a large extent, you are your own boss: you can devise your own work schedule and you can decide what research you want to be involved in. There are also good opportunities for travel. For example, I've spent periods working in New Zealand and Australia, and in the past year I've been on study trips to Holland, Australia and Ireland.

'One of the difficulties of the job is the high degree of competition for research grants. You need to be very self-motivated and be willing to persist, despite rejected research papers and failed grant applications! The pay is reasonable for a scientific job; starting salaries for researchers with PhDs and for junior lecturers are quite good, and better than in government research institutes, although prospects at higher levels are more limited.'

What are your plans for the future?
'In terms of research, increased involvement in international research projects in wildlife management and biodiversity conservation, and in particular trying to understand better the human aspects of many environmental and wildlife-related conflicts.'

Case study 4

GROOM

Karen Rushton-Wright works as a groom at the Northern Equine Therapy Centre in Rathmell, North Yorkshire. The centre has a swimming pool for horses, plus a solarium and equine veterinary facilities. Karen has been working with horses for the last 12 years, since leaving school at the age of 16.

What's a typical day like?
'My day starts at 8.00am when my colleague and I begin by mucking out on average 15 horses. The number of horses does vary depending on the season and the number of veterinary 'in-patients' there are. We then give the horses water and hay, before turning the older ones out into the fields.

'At 9.00am it's our turn for breakfast. First job after breakfast is to work the racehorses. This involves either exercising them on the road or cantering them in the field. When we finish their exercise we untack them, then put their rugs back on.

'The swimmers are next and they are put on the horse walker to warm up. This gives us a chance to "skip out" their boxes

I enjoy working as a groom because you don't have the responsibilities you would have if you ran your own yard.

(remove any droppings) before we swim them. After they've swum they dry off under the solarium before being rugged up and returned to their boxes. Most of the horses enjoy swimming, but occasionally you do get one who might dig his hooves in! The horses then get their lunchtime hay before we get our lunch at 1.00pm.

Most of the horses enjoy swimming, but occasionally you do get one who might dig his hooves in!

'The afternoons are spent doing various jobs, including cleaning tack, sweeping and tidying up the yard. At 3.00pm we start to finish off. All the horses need skipping out, and fresh water and hay needs to be laid out. An average day will finish at 4.30pm.'

At what age did you decide that you wanted to be a groom?
'At the age of 4! I used to help out my mum's friend with her horses and ever since have been involved with horses.'

What do you enjoy most about your job?
'The fact that I'm getting paid to do my hobby. I couldn't afford to keep my own horse so this is the next best thing.'

What qualifications do you have?
'I left school at 16 and went to Craven College where I completed my BTEC First Diploma in Horse Management, and the British Horse Society Stage 1 qualification. I then

worked at the hunt kennels, a horse dealers and a stud
before I came to work here at the Equine Therapy Centre.'

What are your plans for the future?
'I enjoy working as a groom because you don't have the
responsibilities you would have if you ran your own yard. You
get days off and the same kind of working conditions you
get when you're employed in other jobs.'

Making up your mind

13

There are many different jobs that involve working with animals and wildlife. So before deciding which career to choose, there are a number of questions that need to be carefully considered and answered.

WHAT ARE THE CAREER OPPORTUNITIES?

Employment prospects working with animals and wildlife are good, with strong growth in a number of specific areas in recent years, especially the environmental field. There are many different career options to consider, as outlined in the earlier sections of the book. For someone with the right attitudes and skills, there has never been a better time to go for a career working in this field.

WHAT ARE THE SALARIES LIKE?

Salaries vary tremendously between the various jobs. Generally not many jobs working with animals or wildlife pay high salaries, so you need to decide how important money is to you.

DO I NEED TRAINING?

That depends on which career you decide to choose. A number of jobs offer training once you have secured the job, but for others the training is intense and competition to gain admission to a course is high. One point that cannot be stressed enough is the importance of work experience. The more work experience you have, the better your chances will be. There are many people out there who have university degrees, so when going for an interview, you need to be able to stand out from the rest. Start getting some experience as soon as you can, even if it means helping out at your local stables once a week or walking dogs for a kennel.

CAN I WORK ABROAD?

There are excellent prospects if you get the travel bug and want to work abroad. The animals and wildlife sector is on the up in many European countries, as well as in the USA, Canada, New Zealand and Australia. There are special rules that apply to working in other countries, so if this is something you are seriously considering, it is best to check with the employment authorities in the country concerned.

Opportunities also exist in less economically developed countries too, especially where large areas of wilderness survive, which support impressive populations of wild animals. However, in these countries pay is very low compared to that in the UK, and you might even be expected to work as a volunteer.

WHAT HOLIDAYS WILL I GET?

If you work for an employer there is a minimum holiday entitlement of 20 days' leave per year. Because of the nature of work with animals, bank holidays are not always guaranteed. If you are self-employed – as a farrier, for

> **DID YOU KNOW?**
>
> The average annual salary for full-time workers in the land-based sector in the UK is £16,000. This is equivalent to £307 per week.

example – you need to plan the best time to take a holiday. This cannot be guaranteed in the summer.

WHAT HOURS WILL I BE EXPECTED TO WORK?

When working with animals and wildlife do not expect to be doing a nine-to-five job. Hours are often unpredictable and vary from day to day. In many jobs you will be expected to work your fair share of unsociable hours and these could be at the weekend. Crises can occur at any time and you might even be expected to be at work late into the evening. Breaks and lunches are not likely to be at set times either, as animals tend not to work to our timetables!

WILL I BE ABLE TO CHANGE CAREER IF I DO NOT ENJOY WHAT I AM DOING?

Once you have embarked on a course of study, it is always possible to change direction in your career. For example, the journalist interviewed on page 38 swapped reporting in war-torn countries for a job looking after rhinos. If you start a job working in one field related to animals or wildlife, this experience might enable you to work in another animal-related job, perhaps with a little more training. It would also count as valuable work experience in its own right.

WHAT ARE THE OPPORTUNITIES FOR RUNNING YOUR OWN BUSINESS?

The business opportunities are good as long as you can provide a product or service that is genuinely needed, or provides a new slant on an existing idea. To be successful in business you will need to be able to think creatively, be prepared to take risks and be willing to sell your ideas to others, not least the bank to secure a loan to get started! There are many examples of people who have made a successful living through running their own businesses in the animal and wildlife sector. But there are also those whose businesses have failed. Despite the success of high-profile UK entrepreneurs such as Sir Richard Branson (the Virgin Group) and Anita Roddick (the Body Shop), starting your own business can be tough and success is far from guaranteed. Many self-employed people work longer hours than those working for an employer, and take home less pay. But the rewards and freedom of being self-employed are hard to put a price on.

14

The last word

After reading this book you should have a much clearer idea of what working with animals and wildlife is all about. You will also be able to judge whether such a career would suit you, although you may still be undecided.

There is a lot more to think about and do before you can finally commit yourself to this particular career route. You should try to follow the advice in the checklist below if you still feel committed to a career in this field:

- Be really clear about *why* you want to work in this field.
- Focus on a few specific job areas that really interest you.
- Discuss things with your parents or carers.
- Talk to as many people as possible who work with animals and wildlife.
- Listen carefully to what others tell you and be realistic about what you can do (but don't put yourself down!).
- Try to carry out some work experience as this is an excellent way of finding out what any job is really like and will make your job applications look stronger.
- Contact the organisations or companies that you are especially interested in working for to get further, more specific information.
- Discuss your options with a careers officer in a careers centre or at your school or college.

- Consider the entry options for your chosen career. Think about whether your existing skills, qualifications and experience will allow you to move into your chosen job area or whether new qualifications are needed.
- Decide whether you can afford to train full time or whether a part-time arrangement, allowing you to earn at the same time, is preferable. Some jobs may come with on-the-job training leading to a vocational qualification.
- Be determined; a lot is possible with a positive mental attitude!

Remember, research is the key to effective decision-making and you will find a wealth of organisations and help listed on the following pages that will help you make the right decisions.

Research is the key to effective decision-making.

Good luck with your career working with animals or wildlife!

ARE YOU PHYSICALLY FIT?

☐ YES
☐ NO

DO YOU HAVE A RESPECT FOR ANIMALS?

☐ YES
☐ NO

ARE YOU READY TO DEDICATE YOURSELF TO
WORKING WITH ANIMALS?

☐ YES
☐ NO

ARE YOU READY FOR HARD WORK, OFTEN WITH
LOW PAY?

☐ YES
☐ NO

ARE YOU PREPARED TO WORK UNSOCIABLE HOURS?

☐ YES
☐ NO

DO YOU HAVE GOOD INTERPERSONAL SKILLS?

☐ YES
☐ NO

ARE YOU ABLE TO WORK WELL WITH THE
PUBLIC?

☐ YES
☐ NO

ARE YOU A GOOD TEAM WORKER?

☐ YES
☐ NO

ARE YOU SELF-MOTIVATED AND KEEN TO LEARN
ON THE JOB?

☐ YES
☐ NO

If you answered 'YES' to all these questions then

CONGRATULATIONS! YOU'VE CHOSEN THE RIGHT CAREER!

If you answered 'NO' to any of these questions then this may not be the career for you

Resources

15

GENERAL CONTACTS

CONNEXIONS
www.connexions.gov.uk

CONNEXIONS DIRECT (ADVISERS)
Tel: 080 800 13219
www.connexions-direct.com

LANTRA
Lantra House
Stoneleigh Park
Nr Coventry
Warwickshire CV8 2LG
Tel: 024 7669 6996
www.lantra.co.uk

Welsh Regional Office
Royal Welsh Showground
Llanelwedd
Builth Wells
Powys LD2 3WY
Tel: 01982 552646
www.lantra.co.uk/wales

Scottish Regional Office
Newlands
Scone
Perth PH2 6NL
Tel: 01738 553311
www.lantra.co.uk/scotland

National training organisation for the environmental and land-based sector.

THE CAREERS PORTAL
www.careers-portal.co.uk

Award-winning online careers resource that is part of the National Grid for Learning, providing a gateway to careers and higher education on the web.

Remember too that search engines such as www.google.co.uk are an excellent way to find a whole range of additional information on job areas that interest you.

CAREERS ADVICE AND INFORMATION

LEARN DIRECT
www.learndirect-advice.co.uk

UCAS ENQUIRIES
UCAS
PO Box 28
Cheltenham GL52 3LZ
Tel: 0870 112 2211
www.ucas.ac.uk

ANIMAL HEALTH AND WELFARE

Getting into Veterinary School by Mario di Clemente (Trotman, 2005)

BRITISH VETERINARY NURSING ASSOCIATION
Suite 11,
Shenval House
South Road
Harlow
Essex CM20 2BD
Tel: 01279 450567
www.bvna.org.uk

ROYAL COLLEGE OF VETERINARY SURGEONS
Belgravia House
62–64 Horseferry Road
London SW1P 2AF
Tel: 020 7222 2001
www.rcvs.org.uk

ROYAL SOCIETY FOR THE PREVENTION OF CRUELTY TO ANIMALS (RSPCA)
Wilberforce Way
Southwater
Horsham
West Sussex RH13 9RS
Tel: 0870 753 0284
www.rspca.org.uk

ANIMAL CARE CHARITIES

DOGS TRUST
17 Wakley Street
London EC1V 7RQ
Tel: 020 7837 0006
www.dogstrust.org.uk

CATS PROTECTION
Tel: 0870 209 9099
www.cats.org.uk

PEOPLE'S DISPENSARY FOR SICK ANIMALS (PDSA)
Whitechapel Way
Priorslee
Telford
Shropshire TF2 9PQ
Tel: 01952 290999
www.pdsa.org.uk

WILDLIFE MANAGEMENT AND CONSERVATION

BRITISH TRUST FOR CONSERVATION VOLUNTEERS (BTCV)
Conservation Centre
163 Balby Road
Doncaster
South Yorkshire DN4 0RH
Tel: 01302 572244
www.btcv.org

COUNTRYSIDE AGENCY
John Dower House
Crescent Place
Cheltenham GL50 3RA
Tel: 01242 521381
www.countryside.gov.uk

COUNTRYSIDE COUNCIL FOR WALES
Tel: 08451 306229
www.ccw.gov.uk

ENGLISH NATURE
Northminster House
Peterborough PE1 1UA
Tel: 01733 455000
www.english-nature.org.uk

ENVIRONMENT AGENCY
Rio House
Waterside Drive
Aztec West
Almondsbury
Bristol BS32 4UD
Tel: 01454 624400
www.environment-agency.gov.uk

NATIONAL GAMEKEEPERS' ORGANISATION CHARITABLE TRUST
PO Box 3360
Stourbridge DY7 5YG
www.gamekeeperstrust.org.uk

NATIONAL TRUST
PO Box 39
Warrington WA5 7WD
Tel: 0870 458 4000
www.nationaltrust.org.uk

ROYAL SOCIETY FOR THE PROTECTION OF BIRDS (RSPB)
The Lodge
Sandy
Bedfordshire SG19 2DL
Tel: 01767 680551
www.rspb.org.uk

SCOTTISH NATURAL HERITAGE
www.snh.org.uk

THE WILDLIFE TRUSTS
The Kiln
Waterside
Mather Road
Newark
Nottinghamshire NG24 1WT
Tel: 0870 036 7711
www.wildlifetrusts.org

WORLD WILDLIFE FUND (WWF-UK)
Panda House
Weyside Park
Godalming
Surrey GU7 1XR
Tel: 01483 426444
www.wwf-uk.org

THE ANIMAL AND WILDLIFE BUSINESS

ASSOCIATION OF BRITISH RIDING SCHOOLS
Office No 2
Queens Chambers
38–40 Queen Street
Penzance TR18 4BH
Tel: 01736 369440
www.abrs.org

THE ASSOCIATION OF BRITISH WILD ANIMAL KEEPERS
www.abwak.co.uk

BRITISH DOG GROOMERS' ASSOCIATION
Bedford Business Centre
170 Mile Road
Bedford MK42 9TW
Tel: 01234 273933
www.petcare.org.uk

BUSINESS EYE IN WALES
Tel: 08457 969798
www.businesseye.org.uk

BUSINESS GATEWAY SCOTLAND
Tel: 0845 609 6611
www.bgateway.com

BRITISH HORSE SOCIETY
Stoneleigh Deer Park
Kenilworth
Warwickshire CV8 2XZ
Tel: 08701 202244
www.bhs.org.uk

BUSINESS LINK
Tel: 0845 600 9006
www.businesslink.gov.uk

BRITISH RACING SCHOOL
Snailwell Road
Newmarket
Suffolk CB8 7NU
Tel: 01638 665103
www.brs.org.uk

FARMERS' UNION OF WALES
www.fuw.org.uk

THE FARRIERS' REGISTRATION COUNCIL
Sefton House
Adam Court
Newark Road
Peterborough PE1 5PP
Tel: 01733 319911
www.farrier-reg.gov.uk

THE INSTITUTE OF ANIMAL TECHNOLOGY
5 South Parade
Summertown
Oxford OX2 7JL
www.iat.org.uk

INSTITUTE OF FISHERIES MANAGEMENT
22 Rushworth Avenue
West Bridgford
Nottingham NG2 7LF
Tel: 0115 982 2317
www.ifm.org.uk

INVEST NORTHERN IRELAND
Tel: 028 9023 9090
www.investni.com

THE JOCKEY CLUB
42 Portman Square
London W1H 6EN
Tel: 020 7343 2236
www.thejockeyclub.co.uk

NATIONAL FARMERS' UNION
Agriculture House
164 Shaftesbury Avenue
London WC2H 8HL
Tel: 020 7331 7200
www.nfu.org.uk

NATIONAL FARMERS' UNION SCOTLAND
Rural Centre
West Mains
Ingliston
Midlothian EH28 8LT
Tel: 0131 472 4000
www.nfus.org.uk

SERVICES PROVIDED THROUGH ANIMALS

GUIDE DOGS FOR THE BLIND ASSOCIATION
Burghfield Common
Reading RG7 3YG
Tel: 0118 983 5555
www.guidedogs.org.uk

CVs AND INTERVIEWS

Winning CVs for first-time job hunters by Kath Houston (Trotman, 2004)

Winning interviews for first-time job hunters by Kath Houston (Trotman, 2004)

Winning job-hunting strategies for first-time job hunters by Gary Woodward (Trotman, 2004)